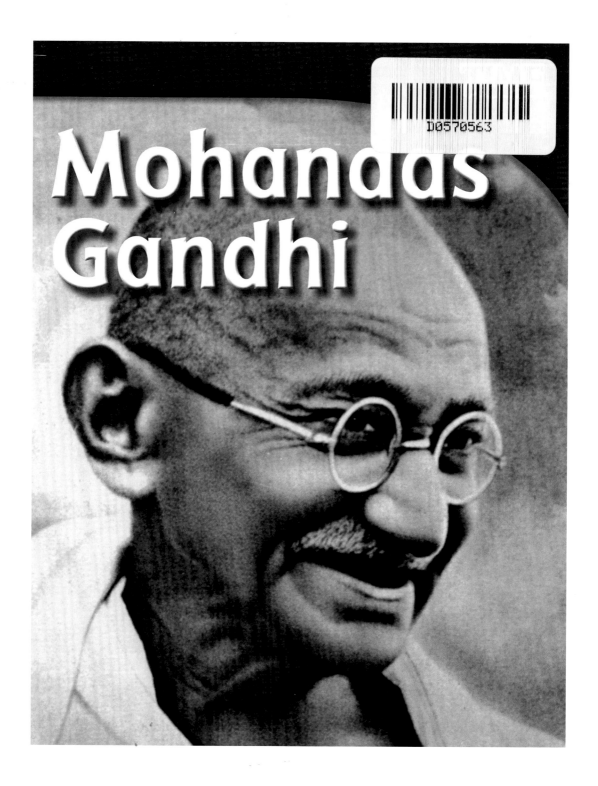

Mohandas Gandhi

Dona and William Rice

Consultant

Timothy Rasinski, Ph.D.
Kent State University

Publishing Credits

Dona Herweck Rice, *Editor-in-Chief*

Robin Erickson, *Production Director*

Lee Aucoin, *Creative Director*

Conni Medina, M.A.Ed., *Editorial Director*

Jamey Acosta, *Editor*

Heidi Kellenberger, *Editor*

Lexa Hoang, *Designer*

Leslie Palmer, *Designer*

Stephanie Reid, *Photo Editor*

Rachelle Cracchiolo, M.S.Ed., *Publisher*

Based on writing from *TIME For Kids*.

TIME For Kids and the *TIME For Kids* logo are registered trademarks of TIME Inc. Used under license.

Teacher Created Materials

5301 Oceanus Drive
Huntington Beach, CA 92649-1030
http://www.tcmpub.com

ISBN 978-1-4333-3682-9

© 2012 Teacher Created Materials, Inc.

Table of Contents

A Child of India

Along the west coast of India, by the Arabian Sea, there is a small town called Porbandar (pawr-BUHN-der). On October 2, 1869, a baby boy was born there. He was named Mohandas Gandhi (mo-huhn-DAHS GAHN-dee).

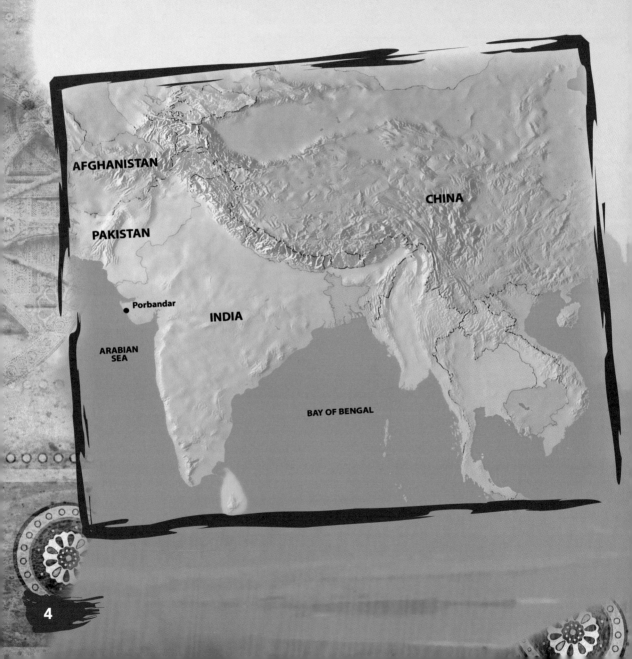

AFGHANISTAN

CHINA

PAKISTAN

● Porbandar

INDIA

ARABIAN
SEA

BAY OF BENGAL

Mohandas's parents influenced him throughout his life.

Mohandas's middle name was Karamchand, after his father's name. His mother's name was Putlibai.

Mohandas's family was good and **honorable**. They lived a strict **Hindu** life. Mohandas's father and grandfather served as **dewans** (dih-WAHNZ), or government advisors. This helped Mohandas to see the importance of public service. His mother was very gentle and **devout**. This helped form the way Mohandas saw the world.

Hindu Temple of Shiva in Chennai, India

What Is Hinduism?

Hinduism is a religion that teaches that all living things are connected. It says that everyone must treat every other living thing with respect and love. Hinduism is a common religion in India.

School Years

Mohandas went to elementary school in Porbandar. Learning was difficult for him. Although he was kind and courteous and tried hard at school, he was labeled a poor student.

When Mohandas was seven, his family moved to another city. His father became a dewan there as well. Mohandas's troubles with school continued. He was very timid and shy, which made things even more challenging. But Mohandas kept trying.

Future Greatness

Mohandas did not stand out during his school years, so no one probably would have guessed that one day he would become a great leader. But one thing happened at school that showed the kind of man he would become. An inspector came to his school to test the students on what they knew. He gave the students a spelling test. Mohandas misspelled a word. His teacher told him to copy the word from a student next to him so that the inspector wouldn't see the mistake. Mohandas would not do it. He knew it was not an honorable thing to do.

Mohandas once said, "The purpose of education is to bring out the best in you."

Mohandas defied his parents by playing with his "untouchable" friend.

Mohandas did not like to see anyone suffer. He was especially bothered by the **caste system** in India. The caste system said that people were born into different **classes**, and they should remain there all their lives. A person from one class should not have anything to do with someone from another class.

Mohandas's family was in the middle class. But Mohandas had a friend who belonged to a lower class known as "untouchable." Hindus believed that having anything to do with an untouchable would pollute their souls. Mohandas's mother forbade him to play with his friend. Mohandas did not want to disobey his mother, but he knew it was wrong to **shun** his friend. He played with him in secret, and he promised himself one day he would work for equality for all Indians.

Untouchables

Mohandas was very troubled by the caste system. He later argued that it was a crime against God and mankind. Those people in the untouchable class were often forced to work in unsafe conditions with trash and other human waste.

Although Mohandas was a good person, he did not always make the best choices when he was young. For a while, he was friends with some young people who often got into trouble. With them, he smoked, stole things, and ate meat, which his religion did not allow.

Mohandas felt terrible about the things he had done. He decided to tell his father everything, apologize, and ask for a punishment. He even asked his father not to blame himself for being the parent of a boy who did such things.

Mohandas's father gave him complete love and forgiveness. Mohandas later said that his father's forgiveness made a big difference in his life.

Mohandas's father

Building a Bond

Mohandas asking for his father's forgiveness was important in many ways. It helped Mohandas to become the best person he could be. He also said that his honest confession and sadness over what he had done strengthened their relationship.

Mohandas as a young man, wearing clothing popular in India and Europe in the 1800s

Marriage

When Mohandas was only 13, he married a 14-year-old girl named Kasturbai (kas-TER-bye). It was the custom in India for people to marry very young. Years later, Mohandas wrote that because of their ages, the wedding simply meant wearing new clothes, eating sweets, and playing with relatives. It took time for the marriage to become the kind that adults have.

Equality of Men and Women

At first, Mohandas believed that he was better than Kasturbai and that it was his job to teach her. He tried to take charge of her. Eventually, he became ashamed of his treatment of her. Over time, he learned that her love and patience taught him many things. He learned also that women and men are truly equal. During his lifetime, he became known for his respect and tender feelings toward women.

Mohandas and Kasturbai, whom he called Ba, enjoyed more than 60 years of marriage. They had four sons together.

A British Colony

At the time that Mohandas was born, Great Britain ruled India. This meant that Indian people, like his father and grandfather, could suggest rules, but the British leaders made the rules. The British people got special treatment, and the Indian people had to pay **taxes** to Britain. Mohandas always thought this was wrong.

In 1885, Mohandas's father died. Mohandas thought he should try to continue his father's work. He hoped he could make a difference.

To begin, Mohandas decided to become a lawyer. He would need to go to England to study law. On September 4, 1888, he set sail for England.

ENGLAND

INDIA

People of Mohandas's caste thought he would be contaminated by crossing the ocean. They released and shunned him from their caste when he decided to sail anyway.

A Young Man

When Mohandas left for England, he was just 18 and a new father. He left his wife and son in India so he could get his education.

Mohandas's first child was born in 1888, just a few months before he sailed to England to study law.

Life in England

When Mohandas arrived in England, he tried very hard to fit in. He bought English clothes and took English classes. He ate English food, but it was tasteless to him. He even took ballroom dancing lessons.

For a long time, Mohandas tried to change himself into an English gentleman. It was very hard, and he was unhappy. But he finally realized something important: it didn't matter what other people thought about him. What mattered was what he thought of himself. When Mohandas realized that, he stopped trying to be something he wasn't.

Vegetarianism

Mohandas was a **vegetarian**. To be a vegetarian means to not eat meat. In England, Mohandas had to eat meat to survive. It took Mohandas a very long time until he found a place that served vegetarian food.

After several years of studying, Mohandas became a lawyer in 1891. He went home to India.

Back in India, Mohandas practiced law for two years. Then, a company that wanted his help with a **lawsuit** in South Africa contacted him with a job. He decided to go to South Africa.

Sad News

Unfortunately, when Mohandas arrived home in India, he learned his mother had died. No one had told him because they didn't want to make life in England any harder for him than it already was.

Life in South Africa

Mohandas left his family and sailed to South Africa for what he thought would be a short time. Once there, he experienced terrible unfairness toward people with darker skin. For example, there were laws in some areas that said people like Mohandas could not vote, walk on the pavement, or own land. Mohandas began to organize the Indians in South Africa. He showed them how to join together to change the laws.

After three years, Mohandas finally returned to India. He told the South Africans that if they needed him, he would come back to help. After just six months, they asked him to come back, and he returned with his family. He continued to support and lead the people in South Africa for nearly 20 more years.

First Hand

Mohandas experienced **prejudice** himself only a week after he arrived in South Africa. He had a first-class train ticket, but a white passenger didn't want Mohandas in her train car. The train officials told Mohandas that he had to ride in third class. He refused. At a train stop, the officials pushed him off the train and kept his luggage. He sat up all night in the freezing train station and tried to figure out what to do. He decided returning to India would be cowardly. The right thing to do would be to finish the job he was hired to do. The next day, he rode another train and continued his business.

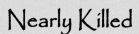

Nearly Killed

Upon returning to South Africa, an angry mob of white people tried to beat Mohandas. They didn't like the changes he was making in their country. One brave English woman stopped them from killing him. Later, government leaders wanted to put the mob in jail, but Mohandas refused to press charges. He wanted to stop the cycle of hatred.

Mohandas's leadership helped to improve the lives of South Africans, such as these miners in the early 20th century.

In South Africa, Mohandas began to change the way he lived. He got rid of many of his belongings. He used only what he needed and lived very simply. He washed his own clothes and cut his own hair. He lived a life of service.

On September 11, 1906, Mohandas spoke at a large meeting. He told the people about **satyagraha** (SUHT-yuh-gruh-huh). *Satyagraha* is a Hindi word that means **nonviolent resistance**. He wanted the people to join him in the nonviolent resistance to unfair laws. It was this nonviolent resistance that made Mohandas well known around the world and helped him to accomplish the changes he wished to make.

Because of his work, Mohandas was often jailed. But in 1914, many of the worst laws were changed. Mohandas had led the people to victory!

Fasting

A *fast* is when a person does not eat for a long period of time. Mohandas fasted so that others would pay attention to his cause. During his career, he led 14 fasts.

The Great Soul

In 1914, Mohandas and his family finally returned to India. Mohandas started building centers for people to learn his way of life and to serve their communities. He also gathered support for satyagraha.

The people of India were still under British rule. Many of the British laws were unfair to Indians. Mohandas taught the people about satyagraha in order to change what was unfair. They worked for one cause after another. Between 1918 and 1919, new laws took away even more freedoms across all of India. When Mohandas—now called **Mahatma**—began to work against the unfair laws, he captured the attention of everyone in India and much of the world. The people of India were now working for their country's independence.

Mahatma

Mahatma (muh-HAWT-muh) is a Hindi word that means *great soul*. During his time in South Africa, Mohandas began to be called *Mahatma*. That is because he lived a life of honor, service, humility, and leadership.

There were many important events during Mohandas's years in India. One of the best remembered is the Salt March of 1930. Britain charged the Indians a tax on salt, and only the British were allowed to make the salt for the Indians. So, Mohandas led a large group of people on a 200-mile march to the Arabian Sea. There, they made their own salt by **evaporating** sea water.

Mohandas continued his work, even though he was often jailed and threatened. But, in 1947, he proved how powerful satyagraha was. After 200 years of British rule, India became a free country!

Nonviolence

Mohandas said, "Nonviolence does not mean making peace. On the other hand, it means fighting bravely and sincerely for truth and doing what is just…. Satyagraha works on the principle that you make the so-called enemy see and realize the injustice he is engaged in."

Mohandas led marches to protest unfair laws.

The Most Important Thing

Mohandas's grandson, Arun Gandhi, was asked by the authors of this book what would be the most important thing to include in the book. He said it is important for students to know about his grandfather's use of anger management. When Mohandas was angered by an injustice, he used his anger as energy to make a difference. He didn't do foolish things because of his anger. This, Arun Gandhi said, is important for all people to learn and practice.

Because of his work, Mohandas had many admirers. But he also had enemies who objected to his teachings and way of life. On January 30, 1948, Mohandas was leading a prayer meeting. An angry Hindu man, who still believed in the caste system, shot and killed Mohandas.

People around the world mourned his death. They could not believe that such a great and peaceful leader had died so violently.

Mohandas was inspired by the many books and articles he read.

The Nonviolence of the Brave

Shortly before he was killed, Mohandas said, "If someone killed me and I died with a prayer for the **assassin** on my lips... then alone would I be said to have had the nonviolence of the brave."

"My life is my message." That is what Mohandas Gandhi once said. He believed that everything he did could make a difference, and he wanted to change things for the better. In India and around the world, millions of people believe he did.

Still Making a Difference

The satyagraha practiced by Mohandas Gandhi has been copied by other great leaders since his time. Dr. Martin Luther King Jr. of the United States and Nelson Mandela of South Africa both followed Mohandas's example to help bring equality to all people in their countries.

Time Line

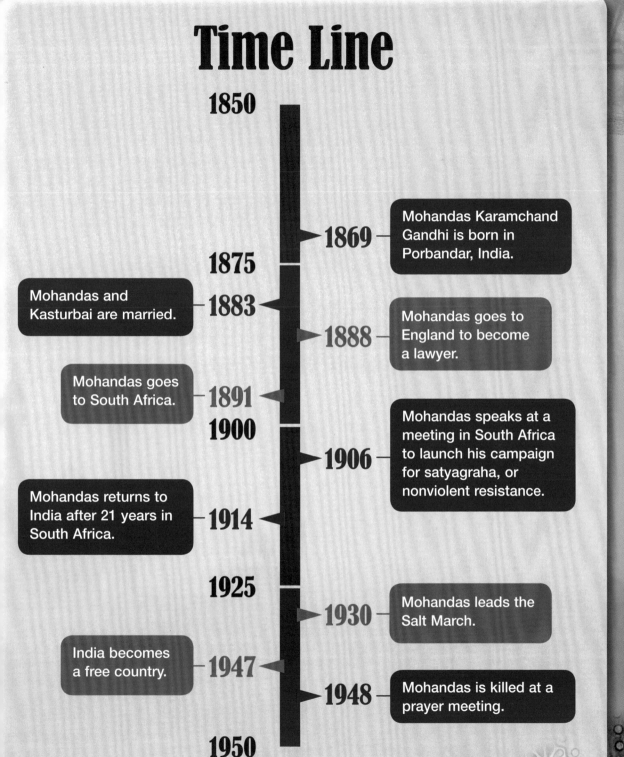

1850

1869 — Mohandas Karamchand Gandhi is born in Porbandar, India.

1875

Mohandas and Kasturbai are married. — 1883

1888 — Mohandas goes to England to become a lawyer.

Mohandas goes to South Africa. — 1891

1900

1906 — Mohandas speaks at a meeting in South Africa to launch his campaign for satyagraha, or nonviolent resistance.

Mohandas returns to India after 21 years in South Africa. — 1914

1925

1930 — Mohandas leads the Salt March.

India becomes a free country. — 1947

1948 — Mohandas is killed at a prayer meeting.

1950

Glossary

assassin—a person who kills someone for political reasons

caste system—a process that was once commonly followed in India in which people are born into different classes where they are said to stay, unable to move higher in class during their lifetimes

classes—different groups or ranks of people in a community

devout—devoted to religion

dewans—the word in the Hindi language for government advisors

evaporating—turning from liquid into vapor because of heat, usually from the sun

Hindu—a person who practices the religion called Hinduism

honorable—living with honesty, integrity, and morals

lawsuit—the legal action made against a person or company, often for money

Mahatma—a title given to a great spiritual leader, meaning "great soul" in the Hindi language

nonviolent resistance—to go against unfair laws or ideas in a peaceful manner in order to change things for the better

prejudice—to be unfair against someone without a good reason

satyagraha—a Hindi word that is best translated into English as *nonviolent resistance*

shun—to avoid or ignore

taxes—money paid to the government

vegetarian—a person who does not eat meat

Index

About the Authors

Dona Herweck Rice grew up in Anaheim, California, and graduated from the University of Southern California with a degree in English and from the University of California at Berkeley with a credential for teaching. She has been a teacher in preschool through tenth grade, a researcher, a librarian, and a theater director, and is now an editor, a poet, a writer of teacher materials, and a writer of books for children. She is married with two sons and lives in Southern California.

William Rice grew up in Pomona, California, and graduated from Idaho State University with a degree in geology. He works at a California state agency that strives to protect the quality of surface and ground water resources. Protecting and preserving the environment is important to him. He is married with two children and lives in Southern California.